D1134840

ROYAL DEESIDE

A pictorial souvenir

NESS PUBLISHING

2   The Royal Bridge over the River Dee at Ballater. This is the fourth bridge here, the previous three having all been swept away.

ROYAL DEESIDE

Welcome to Royal Deeside!

Even in a country so blessed with dramatic landscapes, some areas stand out as exceptional. Even by Scotland's high standards, the slice of Aberdeenshire that lines the course of the River Dee has a reputation for scenic splendour that many believe sets it apart. There are so many different forms of landscape in Scotland that it is impossible, foolish even, to credit any one part of the country as the 'best' or the most beautiful; and yet a few corners of the land have that magic ingredient that imbues them with some facet of character or combination of features that marks them out as special.

Perhaps it is that Deeside tells a complete story, takes one on a journey (quite literally) from mountain spring to waiting sea, revealing the ages and stages of a process that so dynamically shapes the land and holds the fortunes of its inhabitants in its watery hand. As rivers go, it does not rank high in terms of length – 85 miles – but few if any others start in such dramatic or remote surroundings. The Wells of Dee are 4,000ft up in the Cairngorm Mountains, a short distance from which the infant burn falls over a near-vertical corrie edge and crashes down into the Larig Ghru, that huge glacial trench that cuts right through the Cairngorms. Up here in this tundra world rare plants grow and rare birds live, their arctic abode becoming less and less what they need as the climate warms. Yet for now moss campion and mountain saxifrage, the ptarmigan and the dotterel can still be seen.

Deeside begins here. 1220m/4000ft up in the Cairngorm Mountains near the summit of Braeriach, even in June the headwaters tumble through snow at the top of the Falls of Dee.

As the Dee matures into a larger river, fed by countless tributaries born of other mountain crannies, it descends into a glen of many colours and textures: heather and pine, rock and bracken, a different world into which humankind has roamed for millennia. Archaeological evidence shows that people have settled on the banks of the River Dee since Mesolithic times: as the ice receded and flora and fauna returned, people soon followed. The oldest known settlement is at Birkwood where Mesolithic micro flints over seven thousand years old have been found. Around 2000BC tribes of Picts and Celts arrived in the area and in 300AD the Romans came. So many episodes in Scotland's history have taken place here. The first church in Scotland dedicated to St Andrew was built near where Braemar Castle stands today. And speaking

of Braemar, Malcolm Canmore camped near where the village now stands while on his way to confront the infamous Macbeth. The battle took place further down Deeside at Lumphanan in 1057 and Macbeth was defeated.

Most famously of all, midway along Deeside in the shadow of Lochnagar mountain, lies Balmoral Castle, summer home of the Royal Family: Queen Victoria and Prince Albert's

6 The ptarmigan, seen here in winter plumage, is a rare bird of the high Cairngorms.

passion for the area is what put the 'Royal' into Royal Deeside. Their holiday at the Balmoral Estate in 1848 marked the beginning of a life-long love affair with the region. Their decision to buy and develop Balmoral Castle had a profound effect on the development of the area. In each of Banchory, Aboyne, Ballater and Braemar most of the important buildings were built in the Victorian era. Her influence can still be experienced in the Victorian Heritage trail.

This book follows the river from source to sea, thus making the 85-mile journey from west to east, with occasional detours to north and south to take in places of interest that are within Royal Deeside's sphere of influence. So now, whether you are a visitor or a resident, let this pictorial tour remind you of, or prepare you for, the best that this glorious river-world has to show.

Moss campion flowering on the Cairngorms plateau at around 1220m/4000ft.   7

8 This grand vista shows the mountain setting in which the Dee begins. Taken from the Sron na Lairige (the slopes of Braeriach), we look south down the Larig Ghru, the great glacial valley that

carves its way through the Cairngorms. The peak at the end of the ridge on the left is Carn a' Mhaim (1037m/3402ft), while on the other side of the glacial trench is the Devil's Point (1004m/3294ft).

10 Left: the summit of Braeriach (1296m/4252ft), not far from the source of the Dee.
Right: the dotterel is a scarce summer visitor to mountain areas in Scotland, mainly the Cairngorms.

The rugged end of Deeside: from a gully near the summit of Braeriach, the view across the uppermost part of the Dee's course to Cairn Toul (1291m/4236ft) rising above Lochan Uaine.

12 A few miles into its journey and having turned east, the river reaches the Linn ('gorge pool') of Dee, seen here with winter volume of water rushing through. Queen Victoria opened the bridge in 1857.

A north-westerly view from near Inverey of the high Cairngorms at their magnificent winter best. **13**
On the left is the Devil's Point and on the right Cairn Toul.

14 Mar Lodge. The huge Mar Lodge Estate, owned by the National Trust for Scotland, is recognised as one of the most important nature conservation landscapes in the British Isles.

Amongst the wildlife to be seen are the very rare capercaillie, the most impressive of the grouse
family; and red squirrels, plentiful for now but under constant threat from encroaching grey squirrels.

16 The village of Braemar is in the highest parish in Scotland. This westerly view from Creag Choinnich shows that it is located where Glen Clunie (coming in on the left) joins Deeside.

Glen Clunie leads to Glen Shee, one of Scotland's premier skiing destinations. **17**

18 Braemar is most famous for the annual Braemar Gathering, always held on the first Saturday in September. It is a magnificent pageant of marching bands and highland games.

The village itself is very attractive with a number of interesting features. **19**
Here, the bridge over Clunie Water is on the left and the War Memorial is on the right.

20 Clunie Water tumbles (and frequently races) through Braemar on its way to join the Dee.

The landscape of Creag Choinnich, the hill just east of Braemar from which the photo 21 on p.16 was taken. It is a relatively easy and very rewarding walk from the village.

22 It also provides a good vantage point for looking down on Braemar Castle which John Erskine, Earl of Mar (1558-1634) started building in 1628. It is open to visitors in summer.

Again from Creag Choinnich, this is Invercauld House, at the heart of the Invercauld Estate. **23**
It occupies approximately 200 square miles of spectacular Deeside scenery.

24 Near the top of the ridge on the northern edge of Deeside, the expansive view into Glen Gairn opens up. The Gairn is a tributary of the Dee, the confluence of the two rivers being a few miles further east.

26 The old Brig o' Dee between Braemar and Crathie, looking its best having just been restored. Above is the summit of Lochnagar, of which more later.

A little further downstream, this suspension bridge provides an interesting contrast in style. **27**
It leads to the Ballochbuie Forest, one of the oldest stands of Caledonian pines.

28 There have been several centres of worship in Crathie going back to the 6th century. Queen Victoria laid the foundation stone of today's Crathie Kirk, which was completed and dedicated in 1895.

Just across the Dee from Crathie is the Royal Lochnagar Distillery. It was granted a Royal Warrant **29**
of Appointment by Queen Victoria in 1848. Guided tours are available to visitors.

30 Balmoral Castle, the ultimate symbol of what put the 'Royal' into Deeside. It has been a royal castle for 160 years. Queen Victoria and Prince Albert signed the lease in February 1848.

They soon began negotiations to buy and in June 1852 Prince Albert concluded the purchase. Plans **31** were then drawn up for a larger castle to replace the original. The castle of today was completed in 1856.

32 We return now for another look at Glen Gairn, first seen on pages 24–25. This view looks the other way, back towards Deeside.

Gairnshiel Bridge crosses the Gairn burn. This handsome structure was built in 1751. **33**
The Gairn meets the Dee just west of Ballater.

34 The Old Royal Station in Ballater saw a century of service from 1866 to 1966. It was the nearest station to Balmoral and consequently saw much Royal patronage in its heyday.

Today it serves as the Tourist Information Centre and a museum that recreates railway scenes of **35** the Victorian era. Here, the porter appears to be struggling with some of the Royal luggage.

36 A recent addition to the collection is this superb reconstruction of Queen Victoria's railway carriage.

The stunning interior of the carriage. A soundtrack recreates an imagined 37 conversation anticipating their return to Balmoral.

IN DEFENS

NEMO · ME · IMPUNE · LACESSIT

BY APPOINTMENT

ICH DIEN

BY APPOINTMENT TO
HRH THE PRINCE OF WALES
DUKE OF ROTHESAY
BAKERS AND CONFECTIONERS
CHALMERS BAKERY LIMITED

38 Many businesses in Ballater have Royal Warrants which permit them to carry the relevant coats of arms on their premises. Queen Elizabeth II's coat of arms is on the left.

Glenmuick Parish Church dominates the green in the middle of the village. **39**

40 Beautiful Glen Muick runs south-west from Ballater, climbing into the White Mounth, an outlier of the main Cairngorms range. The Lochnagar massif dominates the horizon.

The high point towards the left is Cuidhe Crom, one of the subsidiary tops of Lochnagar. The actual summit is over to the right but hidden in this view.

42 Loch Muick, the largest loch in the Cairngorms, lies at the head of the glen. On a cloudless day the water really is this colour. Broad Cairn (998m/3274ft) towers above.

Lochnagar in its usual winter garb, but on an unusually bright and clear day. 43

44 A close look at the near-vertical drop from the summit plateau of Lochnagar into the corrie below. For comparison, this corrie can be seen towards the right of the picture on pages 40-41.

From a little further round the corrie rim, this is the view down into Lochnagar, **45** the corrie lochan from which the mountain takes its name.

46 Looking east from near the summit, Deeside stretches away into the distance. The peak in the middle distance with an obvious path going up it is Meikle Pap.

And finally, walkers reach Cac Carn Beag, the little tor that forms the very top of Lochnagar at **47**
1155m/3789ft. This area is part of the huge Balmoral Estate which extends to just over 50,000 acres.

48 The view down from Lochnagar really captures the essence of Deeside. Invercauld House and Brig o' Dee can both be seen – compare this picture with pages 23 and 26.

Similarly, from Broad Cairn we now see Loch Muick from on high – compare with p.42. **49**
Mount Keen, Scotland's most easterly Munro, looms on the horizon.

50 Left: a quaint survivor at Cambus o' May – this old AA call box has been beautifully restored.
Right: a typical Deeside Christmas card scene.

About three miles east of Cambus o' May, Loch Kinord in the Muir of Dinnet Nature Reserve makes **51** a fine sight to the north of the A93. A way-marked trail goes around the loch, starting at Burn o'Vat.

52 Autumn comes to the pretty Deeside village of Aboyne, founded in 1671 by the first Earl of Aboyne. The gates lead to the Green of Charlestown, home of the village's Highland Games since 1867.

Aboyne-Dinnet Parish Church on a winter afternoon. It is situated at the opposite end of **53** the Green of Charlestown from the view opposite.

54 Glen Tanar runs south-west from Aboyne. This is the Water of Tanar near the top of the glen, looking south to Mount Keen (939m/3081ft).

Winter can last a long time on Deeside. This beautiful scene at Potarch was recorded in early March. **55**

56 Just a few miles north of Deeside is Tomnaverie recumbent stone circle, built around 2500BC. This is a type of monument that is peculiar to north-east Scotland, 'recumbent' referring to the stone which is placed

horizontally between two uprights – just left of centre. The purpose of this arrangement is unclear, although here the three stones frame the full moon around midsummer at the limit of its movement across the sky. **57**

58 Back in Deeside we come to Kincardine O'Neil, the oldest surviving village on Royal Deeside, having been established at the crossing of two ancient routes. This is the Old Smiddy.

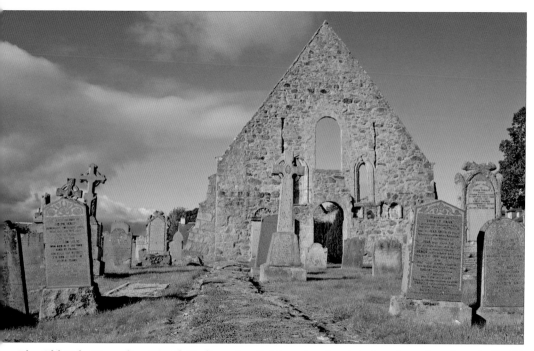

The Old Kirk, Kincardine O'Neil. Dedicated to St Mary, the church is thought to have been built **59** around 1338. Despite renovations in 1799 and 1830 it was replaced by a new building in 1862.

60 A spectacular dawn over Torphins, a north Deeside village, with the Hill of Fare beyond.

Of the hills to the south of Banchory, the tor-topped peak of Clachnaben (589m/1932ft) is the **61** most dramatic. Climbing it makes a rewarding and not too strenuous walk of about three hours.

62 Left: Banchory High Street showing West Parish Church and the Burnett Arms. Right upper: Burnet Arms Hotel sign with horn motif. Right lower: pestle and mortar above the chemist's door.

A lovely display of heathers at the Gordon Highlanders' Memorial in Banchory. **63**

64 The Falls of Feugh are a short walk from the centre of Banchory. The footbridge is a popular place for spotting salmon leaping. This is the view downstream towards Banchory.

The main body of the falls is on the upstream side of the bridge. **65**
The burn is the Water of Dye, on its way to join the Dee.

66 Just east of Banchory, Crathes Castle, with its late 16th-century tower house and later additions. A National Trust for Scotland property, it runs an active programme of events.

Crathes is famed for its wonderful Arts and Crafts gardens and here we see **67**
an array of flowers in one of the greenhouses.

68 Summer colours in the herbaceous borders at Crathes Castle Gardens. In all they cover 3.75 acres and are divided into eight square compartments each of which has a different character.

The Deeside Railway opened to traffic on 8th September 1853 and closed in 1966. A section has **69** been restored and trains run from Milton of Crathes to the outskirts of Banchory.

70 Deeside has a great wealth of castles. Here we see Drum Castle, with its 13th-century tower house, adjoining Jacobean mansion house and Victorian additions.

The tiny but delightful chapel that stands in the grounds of Drum Castle. **71**
It can still be used for weddings.

72 Nearing journey's end: the River Dee has completed most of its 85-mile course as it approaches Aberdeen. From Tolohill to the south-west of the city we see the river spanned by the Bridge of Dee.

Aberdeen, the Granite City, is Scotland's third largest with a population of approximately 210,000.

74 Near the city centre the elegant Wellington suspension bridge of 1831 remains in use for pedestrians only, thus making it the most pleasant way to cross the Dee in Aberdeen.

Probably the most defining view of Aberdeen is this one, from Castlegate, **75** looking down Union Street with the Townhouse taking centre stage.

76 Down by the mouth of the Dee is Foot Dee ('Fittie'), the old fishing village district of the city. Many of the houses are built around traffic-free squares, making for an oasis of urban calm.

What's more, it is only a stone's throw from Fittie to Aberdeen's magnificent and extensive beach. 77

78 This is the business-end of the Dee, full of craft of all description, many of which serve the oil industry. Victoria Bridge marks the inner limit of the harbour.

Finally, a birds-eye view of Aberdeen harbour. Victoria Bridge can be seen towards the right, **79** beyond which Scotland's most regal river melts into the North Sea.

Published 2010 by Ness Publishing, 47 Academy Street, Elgin, Moray, IV30 1LR
Phone/fax 01343 549663 www.nesspublishing.co.uk
Reprinted 2012

Text © Colin Nutt
ISBN 978-1-906549-10-7

Front cover: River Dee near Inverey; p.1: greenhouse flowers at Balmoral; p.4: statue at Balmoral;
this page: one of the many places you can buy this book; back cover: Balmoral Castle

For a list of websites and phone numbers please turn over >

Websites and phone numbers (where available) for principal places featured in this book in order of appearance:

Royal Deeside: www.royal-deeside.org.uk
Aberdeenshire: www.aberdeencityandshire.com
Balmoral Castle: www.balmoralcastle.com (T) 01339 742534
Cairngorms National Park Authority: www.cairngorms.co.uk (T) 01479 873535
Ballater: www.ballaterscotland.com (T) 01339 755467
Mar Lodge: www.nts.org.uk (T) 0844 493 2172
Braemar Gathering: www.braemargathering.org (T) 01339 755377
Braemar: www.braemarscotland.co.uk
Braemar Castle: www.braemarscotland.co.uk (T) 01339 741695
Glenshee Ski Centre: www.ski-glenshee.co.uk (T) 01339 741320
Invercauld Estate: www.braemarscotland.co.uk (T) 01339 741224
Crathie Kirk: www.royal-deeside.org.uk (T) 01339 742344
The Royal Lochnagar Distillery: www.discovering-distilleries.com (T) 01339 742700
Old Royal Station: guide.visitscotland.com (T) 01339 755306
Muir of Dinnet Nature Reserve: www.snh.org.uk (T) 01224 642863
Aboyne: www.royal-deeside.org.uk
Tomnaverie stone circle: www.historic-scotland.gov.uk (T) 0131 668 8600